Praise for Susan Thomas's Writing

Silent Acts of Public Indiscretion

Fierce, haunted, urgent, these are poems that could only have been written in the 21st Century, Catastrophe is already around us and more may lie ahead, but here are offerings of stars, coffee, memories, paintings, and words that stubbornly keep dancing on the edge.

 —Joyce Johnson

Susan Thomas's *Silent Acts of Public Indiscretion* clarifies the poet's belief that poems surround us, waiting to be captured. Paris, Italy, imagining death as a bus, visual art, Jewish cooking, and creeping autocracy—these poems merge embodied experience with electric language.

 —Sean Singer

In the Sadness Museum

"Thomas's "museum" is not a place where sadness can be safely contemplated from an aesthetic distance. Her museum's doors are wide open. In poem after risky poem, with humor, flair, and compassion, she pits the power of redemptive art against the ills and evils of the world."

 —Philip Fried

"Lacrimae rerum" wrote Virgil, pointing to the tears at the heart of everything. Susan Thomas has assembled a twenty-first century portfolio in support of that ancient insight. "We are all swimmers," she writes, "in the River of Grief." As that river flows on in these poems, we also find flashes of tenderness and profound empathic imagination, and above all a capacity to endure and to find ways to become more than the sum of our sorrow, anger, disappointment, and fear. As these finely-crafted lyric poems teach us, that capacity deepens us, and is what in another time we might have called the soul.

—Fred Marchant, author of Said Not Said (Graywolf Press)

Among Angelic Orders

"These are stories in which the past permeates the present and in which memories have enough intensity to summon ghosts. Susan Thomas's graceful writing, particularly powerful in the first person, is filled with tender irony and heart."

—Joyce Johnson

The Empty Notebook Interrogates Itself

"Quick, open these pages and meet The Empty Notebook—the enduring nothingness out of which all is generated, the negative capability on which artists thrive, ecstatic world-wanderer, canny literary imitator, driven self-obsessive—as vivaciously and audaciously imagined by Susan Thomas. Pleasures await."

—Jeanne Marie Beaumont

"Giacomo Leopardi, the great Italian poet, once wrote that great works of art, 'even when they give a perfect likeness of the nullity of things always serve as a consolation, rekindling enthusiasm.' That is precisely what Susan Thomas' incredibly original Empty Notebook poems do. By turns ironic, tragic, comic and filled with the paradoxical gusto of pathos, Thomas' poems shows us a way to start from nothing and claim everything. This is a major work in the tradition of Popa and Zbigniew Herbert whose landscape is the imagined world that mirrors, and, more, ironically completes our own."

—Richard Jackson

ALSO BY SUSAN THOMAS

POETRY

State of Blessed Gluttony

The Empty Notebook Interrogates Itself

The Hand Waves Goodbye - chapbook

Voice of the Empty Notebook - chapbook

In the Sadness Museum

Take Five- prose poems by five authors

STORIES

Among Angelic Orders

TRANSLATIONS

Last Voyage: Selected Poems of Giovanni Pascoli
(with Richard Jackson and Deborah Brown)

Silent Acts of Public Indiscretion

Susan Thomas

Fomite
Burlington, VT

ISBN-13: 978-1-953236-43-2

Library of Congress Control Number: 2021944533

Fomite

58 Peru Street

Burlington, VT 05401

www.fomitepress.com

10/212021

For Maeve and Willie,
Irene and Aurora,
and all their wonderful parents.

And, as always, Peter.

The old world is dying and
the new world struggles to be born.
Now is the time of monsters.

—Antonio Gramsci, *Prison Letters*

Contents

III

Acknowledgments

The author wishes to thank the following magazines in which many of these poems first appeared, sometimes in different forms and with different titles:

Atlanta Review: "The Watched Pot"

Arts and Letters: "The Key to Solipsism"

Caprice and Mischief (Red Hen Press): "Weather Update"

Cerise: "Dining Table with Ghosts"

Crab Orchard Review: "Snow White in Exile"

CUTTHROAT: "Self-Elegy," "Aqua Alta"

Jewish Currents: "Indigestion"

Manhattan Review: "The Beautiful Cars"

MARGIE: "In Medias Res"

Marlboro Review: "Listen to the Moon"

Negative Capability: "Washington Heights, 1952" (Awards from Writers Digest, The Writer's Workshop, Tennessee Writers Alliance)

Notre Dame Review: "Windowlight Supper"

Poems & Plays: "The Hand Waves Goodbye"

Southern California Anthology: "Strolling Down the Via Negativa" (2003 Ann Stanford Award from the University of Southern California)

St. Petersburg Review: "The Rose Marble Table," "Disaster"

The Mississippi Review: "History of the Main Complaint" (MR Prize 2011)

Some poems have also appeared in previously published collections. *The Empty Notebook Interrogates Itself* (Fomite Press, 2011): "Washington Heights, 1952"

The State of Blessed Gluttony (Red Hen Press, 2014): "Washington Heights, 1952"

Among Angelic Orders (Fomite Press, 2015): "The Key to Solipsism", "Weather Update", "Dining Table with Ghosts", "Self-Elegy," "Aqua Alta", "The Beautiful Cars", "In Medias Res", "History of the Main Complaint", "The Rose Marble Table," "Disaster"

In the Sadness Museum (Fomite Press, 2017): "Dancing," "Bluster," "Nostalgia," "Coach for the Abyss," "Vacuum," "A Recipe for Art"

Take Five (Finishing Line Press, 2020) "Stifled", "Dancing", "A Recipe for Art", "Aqua Alta", "Gratitude", "The Garden Then and Now"

My gratitude to Marc Estrin and Donna Bister of Fomite for their continued support and enthusiasm.

Thanks always to my husband, Peter Sills, for his patience (ha!) and fortitude, and to Richard Jackson, mentor and genius teacher, in whose e-group many of these poems began. I also thank my fellow e-group members, Barbara Carlson and Deborah Brown, for their astute comments and companionship.

I especially wish to express my deep gratitude to my dear friend, wonderful poet Jeanne Marie Beaumont, for editing everything in this book I couldn't see, and in the process, re-teaching me important parts of spacing, grammar, and punctuation.

I also thank Shaina Ferguson, Maeve Moynihan and Jill Pralle for their sharp eyes and computer skills.

Silent Acts of Public Indiscretion

I

Vacuum

> *Why are there beings at all*
> *instead of nothing?*
> —Martin Heidegger

Why dogs or cats? Why jaguars, rats, parakeets, humans?
    Why not random chromosomes flying apart?
        I want to be vapor, rising like river smoke in the early morning.

We are all these molecules bunched up together, clinging for dear life.
    Why so dear? We might suspend ourselves anywhere,
        careless of feeling, careless of thought.

We could care less about everything if we just learned to repel—going
    our own way to nowhere, for no reason in no time. How lovely to
be nothing—
        no country, continent, cosmos, to which we pledge allegiance.

To be a black hole—still and invisible, timeless in space.

Strolling Down the Via Negativa

No means yes on the Via Negativa.
Black is white, north runs south, rough
feels smooth, down points up. Dogs bark
sweetly on the Via Negativa, perching
on branches to sing in the trees.
Spending is saving and risk is safety.
War is peace on the Via Negativa.
No one grumbles, no one snarls or has
a nervous breakdown. Nobody's
scared here, nobody's weeping.
Courage grows like cancer. Kindness
falls like acid rain on every picket fence.
Nobody dies here, no drive-by shootings,
no cardiac arrests. We're lucky to live here,
ordering take-out and watching TV,
everyone getting rich on this year's tax cuts,
waiting for the shuttles to outer space.
And everyone's in love on the Via Negativa.
Big houses quiver in the sanitized air,
throw open their doors with feckless
abandon, moaning down chimneys,
they lick the stars from the sky.

Open/Shut

And the gesture of closing is always sharper,
firmer and briefer than that of opening.
—Gaston Bachelard

The flower petals slowly open their little fists
to the outside air. The story starts.
I leave my home to travel beyond,
a stranger comes to town.
Nothing happens.
Days later or after that,
the flower flings open its arms.
It flutters in the fickle wind.
The story progresses page by page.
Something happens.
It stops.
The strangers catch each other's eyes,
catch fingers,
cross paths again and again.
They know the pages they've read in the story,
each word bringing another
to the surface.
Petals float
beyond the page.
We know its ending, recognize
how one word, a phrase, an image,
leads us to another—
leads us to its knowable end.

Stifled

What I say to you is never what
I say to you but something else instead.
— Clarice Lispector

I can barely open my mouth.
What comes out is inaudible.
If something would bubble up inside me,
would enter the place that sound begins,
maybe then I would say
what happens between the lines of my breath.

But as it is,
I find nothing to engage my tongue.
I ask you just the same—
hear me.

Crack the shuttered window of my silence.
Pry me open—listen to me shriek
with terror or with laughter.
Let these words make their futile escape.

Alive

I am going to outlive myself.
      Sleep, eat, sleep, eat.
            —Jean-Paul Sartre

After all, these are the best parts of my life.
    Better than going to the bank, the store,
tidying the pillows on the sofa. At night,
    after eating all the fruits I can cut up—
pineapple, pear, apple, orange, I go to bed.
    How cool the sheets are. I'm lying there,
but I'm swimming in a mountain stream. The blankets—
    I am flying on top of them. Then I dream
everything I ever did or tried to do in my waking life,
    but now it's really happening. I remember it all
and more—it unravels before me in my sleep. Then I wake.
    The usual routine—brush, wash, dress. And then,
coffee. Better almost than dreaming. Hot, bitter, milky froth.
    It pulls me from the world of dreams and drops me
            into its white ceramic cup.

Self-Elegy

You will say I kissed strangers, gave
soup to passers-by. You will say I
moved slowly, dropped things. But
will anyone speak of my dreams?
I don't think I ever told them—ruined
landscapes, mutilated trees, children
sinking into the desert. Fish will cry
for me. Frogs will sing like demented
angels remembering snowstorms that
shot from my eyes. My fingers touched
fire, reached for constellations, swam
rivers. My ears heard forests colliding,
buildings collapsing, telephone voices
screaming good news/bad news. I have
won the sympathy of flowers—they
bloom then wither to show me how.
Fish weep for me though I have never
spoken my love of water, my fear of fire,
my obliterating dreams, which bleat their
terrible madness into someone else's
sleeping brain, some innocent among
pillows, to celebrate my unremembered life.

Dancing

When joy left me I kept dancing anyway. I still heard muffled music and, drop by drop, I heard how hope dripped out of my happy life. When laughter came to my mouth I thought—why am I laughing? Sadness came with sickness and the imminent loss of friends. A child disappeared. A full grown man, but still, my child. The news was relentless and always bad. And if occasionally there was good news we didn't trust it. I kept on dancing, and I knew I was holding inside my body whatever was left to keep me going, waiting for something to return.

Hope goes away when
you no longer love yourself.
Dance it back inside.

9/11/16

Downtown, a stiff breeze blows
the heavy clouds across the river
with the passing rain. Uptown

we remember the day, go about
riding the subway or waiting
for the bus, grateful for

the change in weather despite
a scent of future bombs
hanging in the air.

Halloween

Three o'clock pm. Ghosts and goblins wait for dismissal, all of them ready for mayhem. My doorbell rings a dozen times with skeletons craving candy. Out the window, the river burns in a fire of sunshine. Next to the river a flash of white streaks down the bicycle path, crashing into a school bus. Blue lights, red lights, gunfire, sirens. The little ghosts scream from the windows. Eight mangled bicycles lie in the road. I put back the candy, turn on the news, sit down to stare at the screen, at the ghost bikes, and their absence of riders.

Nostalgia—Paris, November 2015

Years ago
we used to stay
in a rundown hotel
on the Rue St. Benoit.

Every night
we came home from cafés
at St. Germain des Prés—or from
the Metro, after nights at

African tango palaces
or Gypsy clubs near République.
We were always tired, a little drunk,
so we took a shortcut

through a street we called the Rue de Merde,
where old ladies in their nightgowns
walked their dogs late at night.
We tried to avoid them in the dark,

like people leaving the Belle Équipe or the Bataclan
last week. Only they weren't laughing or sauntering
down the rue Jean-Pierre Timbaud.
They were screaming, crying, running, falling—

those who could escape. They were avoiding
bullets and corpses. Watching them on the news,
we longed for the quiet nights of old ladies
and their poodles, committing silent acts
of public indiscretion on the innocent streets of Paris.

Coach for the Abyss

*I see life as a roadside inn where I have
to stay until the coach for the abyss pulls up.*
—Fernando Pessoa

The coach stops every day,
almost always with terrible news.
Jeffrey is dead. And Francoise
has dementia. Some rogue
superpower might declare war
on us or maybe we'll attack them.
Sometimes there's news we want
to hear: Kahlil isn't getting deported.
Willie passed his swim test.

I never get on that coach,
no matter how tempting it looks,
all plush seats and clean windows.
You can't imagine where it's going
to take you. I go for the scary subway
or the filthy bus. And I always climb
out the window or sneak out the back.
Keep a low profile. Don't let them
see you coming in or leaving.

Aqua Alta

The siren goes off at 5 am. It blows us awake to the tapping of hammers, to the shouting of workers in the calle below. Putting together platforms for us to walk on today to rise over the Aqua Alta, the high waters. Forget the Rialto market, the Tintoretto at the Doge's Palace. Forget the Accademia. Today only the Tiepelos make sense. Men, women, horses, deities of myth and religion, all swimming and flying and kicking their way to the ceilings of palaces, the heavenly domes of the churches. And of course, the Bellini Madonna in the Frari, if you can make your way through the Piazza. She is ascending to Heaven with angels to boost her. She rises above the Earth, above the air, above the waters, her face losing its years, losing its grief, losing all earthly connection, she rises.

Disaster

Fiona calls from Paris to tell me
she got a call from Tokyo—
they just had a magnitude 9
earthquake that lasted four
minutes, and now they are
waiting for a tsunami to wipe
out some unsuspecting village
and maybe hit the west coast
of the U.S., or at least give
my kids a thrill in California
and Seattle. And isn't Seattle
on some giant fault like the one
in Chile that could go at any time?
But now I hear the tsunami has
already hit somewhere north
of Tokyo. No word yet of damage
and death, but how could they
get off unscathed? They can't.
And we can't. If it isn't earthquakes,
it's fire or terrorists, tornados,
or even a nuclear meltdown.
Aren't we all in some kind of danger,
waiting around for something to
happen? And meanwhile, we're
doing whatever we can to obsess
over things that can't really hurt us:
mortgages, taxes, tuition, apartments,
our next book, next trip, breakfast
lunch, dinner. Nothing that phone

calls from Paris and TV news can't
disrupt, telling us it already happened,
and all of the demons and angels
that sit on the edge of our world, waiting
to drag us back into theirs, are watching
us, holding their breath, letting us fall
forwards or backwards, not knowing
which side is which and how we
got to wherever it is we are now.

At Sea

The rain won't stop. Drizzle. Torrent. Steady slant. It makes every place the same mess of cold, wet, slippery mush. The coffee is bad. Or is it tea? And just like the soup. We drink it anyway, to keep warm. And as we drink, we start to look the same. We are smaller, greyer, long noses shortening, small eyes growing wider. We are all sprouting eyeglasses. The passengers murmur in a moist, quavery monotone. Sky, water, horizon, coffee, tea, soup, passengers. All through the same damp, grey filter.

Still Life

Torrent of rain, you unravel my lungs, pluck flowers perched in
the trees. I slide across the sidewalk, smashing ribs and kneecap.
Is there a tooth in that puddle, next to string beans I was bringing
home? And the calla lilies—so fresh in the store—randomly strewn
in the storm drain.

The Garden, Then and Now

Of course I remember the garden then,
all Zone 3 plants resplendent in their
summer greed and you and I, just past
bloom, as you said, like the poppies,
the daisies, hydrangeas—but if I replanted
them now, twenty years later, you'd see
more tropical flowers, owing to change in
climate, now Zone 5. More ice, more rain,
less snow, or as we called it, poor man's
mulch. But why complain when everywhere
else rain pelts streams to rivers, wind funnels
cars and houses miles away, highways turn
to black ice, sending tractor-trailers sideways
to cause routine ten-car pileups.

The Rose Marble Table

after Matisse

Remember how we sat in the garden,
the darkening sky, the darkening earth,
how three limes on the octagonal table
stood out in the darkening light,
how we talked until we couldn't see
the green leaves beneath our feet
nor the limes on the table,
the octagonal table, its surface
like skin slowly dying in the darkening
day, how we talked of a time when
you'd be gone and I'd sit all alone
in the garden in the dark
with the rose marble table
there in the deep shade of late
afternoon and your skin would be
as cold as the skin of the table,
its octagonal top reflecting the light
that is left at the end of the day,
its pedestal shaped like your arms
that can no longer hold me
up to the tree to reach for the limes
that grew there—limes that we
placed in a bowl on the rose marble table,
where we sat and palmed the green limes
to warm our cold hands until it was dark
and we passed from garden to house
where you lifted me into my bed
near the window and kissed me

goodnight and pulled down the shade
in the dark and I dreamed of
the garden until it was light every day.

for my grandmother,
Fannie Tomshinksy

Windowlight Supper

after Pavese

The disappearing sky has thrown blue all
over the uplands. The hills are blue, the fields,
even the cows and the trees behind them.
I can still pick out twigs and the frozen

apples clinging to their fingers. Deer float up
in the blue, not quite invisible, watching me watch
them eat the frozen apples while I pick at what's left
of my dinner. I can still make out the food

on my plate, blue tomatoes, blue rice, blue onions.
Soon the stars will fling themselves into darkness.
Nothing ever stops. Time makes no difference.
It circles overhead, watching me. I swallow

my dinner and listen to the clatter of plants
and seasons. I stand at the window, envying
the stars for their chummy ways with each other,
for the brilliant lives they lead in the frozen

throat of the cosmos while I hold fast
to warm house, this room with chairs and books
and table holding food I planted last year in
the tipped bowl of garden under this window.

Gratitude

with the words going out like cells of a brain
with the cities growing over us
we are saying thank you faster and faster
—W.S. Merwin

When Muriel got sick she sent me poems.
They were what she was reading to survive.
She felt lucky to be living
and sent poems every day,
many of them Merwin's—
with the night falling we are saying thank you.

I made soup every day and froze it
so she'd always have something to eat.
She asked for favorites and twice that year,
requested shows on Broadway.
I'm so happy, she whispered during *Carousel.*
She sang through *My Fair Lady.*

A second tumor appeared but she was still sending
poems. One year Merwin chose Muriel's
son, Sean, as Yale Younger Poet,
and came to New York
to introduce Sean at his book launch. Merwin
said he'd been lucky, one of few early successes
whose career had survived its good luck.

But our luck was running out as his stretched on
a little longer. Muriel weakened every day,
and she sent the same poem over and over—

Merwin's—while she kept asking for soup.
His poem—*Thanks*—stuck in her head.
And now this poem is for both of them...

with nobody listening we say thank you
we are saying thank you and waving
dark though it is

A Recipe for Art

I'm interested only in expressing basic human emotions—tragedy, ecstasy, doom, and so on—
—Mark Rothko

His dark palette starts in preoccupation with death. He adds irony, chance, a lustful relationship to existing things. Then, the tension of curbed desire, and now we see how blue is held in a world of plum. Brown suspends it in the air, elevates its mood, almost makes it tingle. Brown is resolute. We depend on it to hold giddiness in check, as we heave relief in the heart-thumping leap from a sea of plum that almost swallowed us whole. What kept us in that eternity of plum, was hope, Rothko's last ingredient. Hope, as he said, to make everything endurable.

II

Weather Update

The air's heavy breathing makes me sick,
keeps me up at night with its stench
of freezing sweat and shrieking whispers.
I hate the taste of the rain; it paws me all day.
I hate how the sky leers with its one dim eye

watching us trip the trick wires—
can't it see what we do to each other?
History's boobytrap opens and
bulldozers grind the luckless to dust,
while we slap at misfortune's hold.

My hands are screaming for a chance
to smack this week off the map
and you know next week won't be any better.
They're calling for flurries with suicide
bombers, torrential weeping into the night.

Dreams Are the Sewer of the Soul

after Fernando Pessoa

Who thought our dreams would turn out this way? My dreams are
monstrosities pulling at the corners of my brain. In my last one, a
slimy creature of the sea pulls me down to his domain until I wake
as if asleep, but know nighttime is just a

madhouse made of sleepless
worms that eat what's left of our
impossible dreams.

Fear

Bed, you beckon me to safety, comfort me with pillows, blankets, holding pain at bay. Nights you toss me to the ceiling, roll me to the floor. There's no escape from your surface or my body. And, of course, it's worse outside the window—SUVs crash through plate glass, wind flattens entire islands, people wash down rivers followed by balls of fire ants. The ground shakes buildings into rubble. People shoot into crowds from buildings. Missiles threaten to annihilate us all. No one is safe from anything. And who am I to be scared?

The Watched Pot

Bubbe is cooking a soup.
Beef bones, onions, and celery.
She sits at the stove on a stool
and watches the pot like TV.
So Zeida says, *Tell me what*
is so terrific in this pot?
She shrugs her narrow shoulders.
A boiling pot is an interesting thing.
She remembers how her mother
boiled goose fat down in a pot,
packed it in a gallon jar
and took it to America.
Her sister Sophie had it when
she moved to St. Nicholas Avenue.
Was the jar still on the kitchen shelf,
or could someone have thrown it out?
She sees the incinerator shaft
of her sister Sophie's building,
the jar of *schmaltz* gone down
the chute, the tinkling pieces of glass,
the splattering, shrieking fat in the fire,
the cousins she played with in Kovno,
who missed the boat to America.
Bubbles rise and dissolve in the soup
and my grandmother watches
with her reading glasses on.

Dining Table with Ghosts

after Pierre Bonnard

A substantial meal even for the living, but these
two pick at food like adolescents. Does the girlish
figure matter now? Especially when the tables
are turned and Renée, her suicide, years ago,
a wedding gift to M. and Mme. Bonnard, now
is the life of the party. Relationship has no legality
in death. She gleams like the striped satin tablecloth,
her blonde hair, brilliant against it, her smile sharpens
the silverware, her eyes the luscious plums of every
still life Bonnard has ever painted. And Marthe,
as shadowed in life as she is in death, is used to being
a phantom, a camouflaged presence in every painting,
at every meal, like the Sumerian ghost who told his
friend that death was much like life only grayer. Maybe
it is only memory that shades or brightens, and now
Renée—released to Pierre's imagination by Marthe's
death—has taken her place at the center of the table.

Catastrophe

It happened at night. Everyone knew right away, except the early sleepers. First there were screams from all the apartments—then silence—the streets, the buildings, the absence of traffic. Then stars fell out of the sky, landing, one by one, on the sidewalk, hissing. The fat moon leered down at us, smirking.

No one could sleep. We went into the streets, grieving, shouting our outrage. We were on the news, along with every detail of the catastrophe and how it continued to unravel our lives. Traffic snarled. Buildings had lights on through the night. The stars still sprawled on the sidewalks, losing their light and whimpering.

The moon shook its fist. A whale came up the river as far as 96th street. It was just looking for food, but somehow it calmed us, gave us hope. Something from long ago, from another world to ours. But the stars deflated even further on the sidewalks. The moon's loutish grin began to wane.

Bluster

We huddle at the bus stop against the tunnel of wind that explodes
from the river and grabs at us around the towers. We're bundled
in coats and scarves and hats, too wrapped up to meet each other's
eyes. We're too swaddled to talk until the bus arrives and we start
shedding pieces in the heat. We talk, we laugh, we sneer, and try to
keep our tempers but we can't stop complaining of twisted characters,
hideous speeches, terrible tweets, and even—treason. What will we
do now? Because all of us are helpless and almost glad to bundle
up, get off the bus and hit the wind.

Night Vision

The stars are the informers of the sky.
They need to see everything–why?
                 —Osip Mandelstam

Again the midnight bird brings news to turn the sky around. She pecks at our brains and eats our innards, while above us, the stars twinkle with malice. We carry her excrement in our hearts, straining to hear whatever tidbit turns our stomachs. What next? What next? The bird cackles and tweets, *Fake news! Never happened. Nut job, nut job! Sad.* We cringe at the luster of the stars. Can't they stop their constant harping? Their sharp points stab us while we gobble up each scandal. Vindictive terror spews from every tongue.

Who Loves Our President?

The Chinese loved our president. They loved his yellow hair. They loved his height and width, and especially they loved his voice. They loved how loud he talks and how he says whatever he wants whenever he wants to say it. They loved Melania, too, because she loved their zoo. The Japanese, not so much. They think his hair is funny. They think his voice is funny. They think he is too fat and he speaks without thinking. They are reserving opinion on his wife. The Vietnamese are not saying what they think of our president, or maybe they have no opinion. The Philipinos and the North Koreans think whatever their dictators tell them to think. New Yorkers hate him. That's what he hears from his apartment. *New York hates you. Go away. We hate you.* All day, all night. That's why he plays so much golf.

The Key to Solipsism

The picture is a model of reality.
The picture itself is a fact.
The world consists of fact.
In this picture, Naghma Mohammed,
a six-year-old Afghan girl, who must
marry the son of a man who lent money
to her father, who borrowed it
to pay hospital costs for Naghma's
mother and funeral costs for the baby,
who froze to death because there was
not enough money for wood to heat
their tent. Because Naghma's father could
not pay back the loan with the money
he made teaching quails to sing and
selling them to other refugees in the camp,
he had to sell his daughter as collateral.
I have nothing to say about this picture.
I cannot answer, as Wittgenstein says,
that which makes no sense, but only
state its senselessness. We cannot think
what we cannot think. Therefore, we can
say nothing about that which we cannot
think about. And yet, I cannot stop thinking
about Naghma, or looking at her picture.

Mrs. Roosevelt at Midnight

Dressed in coat and hat, pocketbook on her lap, her statue guards the entrance to Riverside Park at 72nd St. She leans on her stone bench, always there, watchful as in life, guarding the rights of others. Behind her are the little dogs in their designated doggy park. They come all day with their owners, happy to greet her at the entrance, then run free of their leashes. But at night there are few dogs, fewer people. That's when you might see them—narrow heads, narrow haunches, a trotting gait that gives them away as coyotes. Here in the city, they want the night, they want the unwatched dogs in their dog park.

Eight bright eyes glow green. Hungry coyotes stalk dogs but fear her stone eyes.

Worry

My son keeps telling me to move next
winter to the Florida Keys, hiding from
the boomerang effect of coronavirus.
But I tell him I'm worried for him, not me,
with bullets raining down on us,
rain pelleting our streets,
turning them to rivers,
while shotguns, tear gas,
lava leaks, explosions,
spray random targets, random locations
and all of us wondering where to go
when the weather, the language, the hate
attacks our homes and countries,
our food supply. It rolls germs of all kinds,
into the atmosphere, dropping us deeper
and dumber, sleepless and lost.

Listen to the Moon

On the beach a man
talks into his cell phone.
The fat moon rises. She's peevish tonight
dying to tell the world what no one
wants to hear. It's hard
to listen to a bossy moon.
It's hard being a moon
that nobody listens to.
Whatever time has left,
her surface betrays, and
she knows we'd rather hear
lies decked out in elegance
than the frowsy truth.
So the moon, gussied up
in borrowed light, keeps
her mouth shut, mangles
her words on the beach.
The man shouts *I love you*
into his cell phone.
He leers at the face of the moon.
No one can hear her weeping
in the slap of the sea,
the scratch of the sand.

Apex New York

Here we are at the epicenter.
The apex, or maybe just
a fluke in numbers too heavy
to speak. Even our breath
is taken away by an earth
that pays us back for all
the damage we have done,
but still sends us tulips,
daffodils, blooming magnolias,
and other tokens of our
lucky lives. The sun still touches
our forbidden faces. Every day
we cheer, we clap, we bang
pots and pans at seven o'clock
when shifts change at hospitals
and angels pass each other by
under a darkening sky. Dr. Li,
I whisper, Captain Crozier,
all our secret heroes, as though
they could keep us from harm.
We applaud people who can't
stay home—their job is
to care for us all. And
we cheer for ourselves as well,
for still being here to applaud.

Forgetting Time Lost

I never understood how time passes.
—Grace Paley

By the time we all knew
how much time we had lost
it was too late to count it, but

we marked our time with two
seven o'clocks, each day
in our beloved city.

We tried to grab hold of
parts of time, the way we
remembered each day—

You'd have no time for
all our fussing. *Well, ok,*
you said. *Farewell certain years.*

You would have clapped
and yelled loudest of all
putting neighbors into groups

of angels, cheering the living
and mourning the dead, especially
the poor, the unknown, the unlucky.

Where We Are

Our world gets smaller every day,
with fewer familiar things—
no restaurants, theater, opera,
ballet, no extended family.
Are there still ashes in the air
where you are? Or does it smell
of sickness? Are you still running
around or do you stay at home
in bedroom slippers, sneaking looks
outside at budding tulips and
blooming trees, forbidden to us here
because of crowding in the parks.
I go out for a little walk each day, but
steer clear of elevators crowded with
suspicious tenants and their dogs,
which finally keep their distance
as I've always requested, but now
it's because I'm the potential enemy,
not their asthma-inducing dander.
Sometimes friends call, disembodied
voices on the phone. We are grateful
for the remnants of our old lives.
We are grateful for the love
that still hangs in the heavy air.

The Hand Waves Goodbye

The night before its amputation
the hand decided to run away.
It left a trail of fingerprints
all the way down the hall,
exited the automatic doors.
Passed through the garden,
Slapped through marshes,
Smacked at the brush, and
Thumbed a ride on the highway.

It longed for the voice whose
arm was asleep in the hospital bed
who dreamed of a fist asleep
at its wrist, singing a song the hand
used to strum in the sad hours
after the sun had fallen behind
the hills that tip into the pasture.

The voice's feverish song
blew night's sharpness into
the room where music the hand
could no longer make imagined
the wrist that bent to the beat
while it wailed and pounded
the star-pierced sky and it shook
the hand deep into darkness.

for D.L.

III

Sarah's Exile

Lech, lecha. Go. Leave this place.
—God

To tell you the truth
I feel bad for you—
always listening to the words
of someone who doesn't know
what he's talking about
but is sure he's right.
He hears the words
in his head and never listens
to anything.
His God talks to him.
Sounds familiar, no?
Did Abraham listen to me?
By the time we went forth
to a place we could never leave,
he was so full of himself
he made up laws for everyone.
Even the Pharaoh obeyed him.
He sent Hagar, his daughter,
to serve us, gave us land to build
a nation. People followed wherever
we went. Just like you Americans.
What will you do with all these
immigrants headed your way?
Put them in cages? Send them
into exile like Hagar and Ishmael?
Believe me, they won't be you
and if you treat them as strangers,

they'll resent you the rest of your
days together. And your children,
as well, and their children too,
and theirs, and theirs, and so on.

In Medias Res

Back from getting the paper
you notice the lock's been changed,
the furniture moved—the tweed sofa
turned black leather, the rocking chair
a hassock, the parakeet a hamster.
And the people who used to live here,
the family you used to know as
well as your fingers and toes?
Well—isn't this man in corduroy
at least familiar? Maybe so—or not—
have ten years passed? Things aren't
as they were. But a rhythm begins and
we dance, we eat what's on the plate,
go about our business pretending we
know what's going on in our head,
even though we know it isn't ours.
The shirt fits the man, the dance fits
the music even though it doesn't
move us. We go in and out the door,
raise the shade in the morning, shower
and anoint our strange bodies with
familiar lotions. The world spins around
itself, as do we, but something out there
far away needs to be acknowledged.

Rachel and Leah and Jacob and Bilha and Zilpa

We planned it together.
Rachel and I fell in love
with a stranger/not a stranger,
a cousin from our father's sister,
a kind and gentle man—I knew
he would never love me. He would always
love Rachel, my beautiful younger twin.
I was lumpy and had one eye
that wandered on its own. The younger girls
were part of it, too—Bilha and Zilpa,
daughters of our father's slaves.
They knew they'd be placed as servants—
why not with us, their sisters?

Of course he adored Rachel. He worked
seven years in order to marry her,
but my father tricked him, dressing me
in heavy veils to marry me off, the ugly daughter
no one would ask. When Jacob found me in his bed,
he worked seven more years to keep Rachel in the bargain.
I had six sons in those early years, and my hapless,
beloved daughter. Rachel couldn't conceive, so
she had Bilha, as her handmaid, give herself to Jacob.
Rachel claimed the babies, two sons, as her own,
then had one of her own.
Joseph was a wonderful child, Jacob's favorite.
My boys were all thugs—ruffians at best,
jealous and ready to fight for any reason.
While I cooked and washed and kept our tents,

I let them raise themselves,
but Rachel spent hours
talking to Joseph, telling him stories,
showing Jacob how smart the boy was.

Everyone loved Rachel, her beauty,
her sweet voice, even her laziness.
Nobody loved me, especially Jacob.
But who do you think ended up
buried next to him in the caves?
Was it Rachel, his beloved?
No—she wandered off in the desert when
we moved our tents to Bethlehem. I told her
the second child she expected was close.
What was she thinking when she went off

with Joseph and her nurse? The baby
was born, she died. End of Rachel's story.
They buried her somewhere on the road.
And I? When my time came, they put
me in the tomb of the patriarchs with Jacob
next to me when his time was up.
Not Rachel, not Bilha, his second favorite,
not Zilpa—all prettier, more loved than I was.
Not them, but I, Leah, next to him at last.
For eternity, whether he liked it or not.

Naomi Asks a Question

Was I right to take these girls? I ask myself.
I always ask myself—right or wrong? Which is it?
I am impulsive. Once I listened to my husband,
but now he is dead. They are all dead. My two sons,
their father—everyone but these girls, the wives
of my dead sons, daughters of the Moabite king.
My husband settled us here, escaping famine in Judea.
But now I must return to my own land, my own people.

The problem is the girls, the daughters-in-law.
They wanted to come with me, so I wouldn't be in danger,
an old woman alone, vulnerable to thieves, and so
at first I said yes—after all, I loved them both
as my own and was glad to have them with me.
But then I thought about it—I always change my mind—
and I saw it wasn't right, bringing them into the unknown,
a strange place, among strangers who might not accept them.
Of course they could go back to their parents. I told them so.
And one left, Orpah, the wife of my older son. But Ruth,
she stayed, she wouldn't leave me. We walked barefoot
together, holding hands all the way to Judea. The famine was over.

There were plenty of fields to glean. We met Boaz,
a kinsman of my husband, a man my own age,
a wealthy landowner. And here I must stop again.
I must ask myself again if I did the right thing. Who knows?
I encouraged my young daughter-in-law to go to Boaz at night
in the threshing floor. I told her to lie with him, make him feel
young again. He was kind, still handsome, a vigorous man.

I told her to open her robe, to stay with him. Was I wrong?
I'm asking myself, knowing what came of it all.
They married, and on their wedding night, they pleased
themselves until the sun shone. Then Ruth rose to get breakfast.

She brought Boaz his gruel and saw him still sleeping,
with a sweet smile on his still handsome face. But she was wrong.
He was dead. I blame myself. I brought it on.
But if I am guilty, I also ask what to say for
the child of their wedding night and for his son, Jesse,
and Jesse's son David, and David's son Solomon—
and Ruth, who lived to raise them all, no stranger
in a foreign land, but the grandmother of kings.

Snow White in Exile

Mother, I dream of dragonflies
and insect wings, the furry undersides
of bats. I dream of poison figs
and silver spiders. I dream of you
in your tower, stirring potions
to preserve your famous beauty.
The little men don't know
that every time I let you in
it's not because you trick me,
but that I hope you'll take me home.

But Mother, I know what happens.
I've seen it in your mirror: the poison apple
locked in my throat, the ugly grieving dwarves,
the prince who brings me back to life
with ardent, sloppy kisses.
And Mother, I know my joyous
and terrible wedding day.
The iron slippers lie ready.
They'll force them on your pretty feet.
You will dance for us and die.

Mother, I'll dream for all my life
of spells, infusions, nightshade,
entrails in glass jars, ground beetles,
not of the mother who wished me
white as snow and red as blood,
and died when I was born.
I'll dream of your hand in mine

as we climb the tower stairs.
I'll dream of the smiling mirror
and your sweet breath
kissing my cheek like a feather.

Giving Away

My hand is something I take for granted
I forget to thank it for what it can hold
or let go of.
—Cora Brooks

Rushing through the airport,
newly refurbished, extended, filled
with people I never saw before,
I caught poems on the wall, twelve
of them, then slowed my steps, let
my nervous eyes fill with hope.
If poems could appear out of nowhere,
maybe the air would hold me aloft
even in this snowstorm. There
they were—your poems—written by
someone I know from parties, rallies, vigils.
Friend of my friend, Grace,
friend of my friend, Anne.
The poems held your presence, strong but ethereal,
the way you gave purpose to each occasion.

But it was your death that put you
firmly in my mind. There had been little strokes
that left you wobbly in gait and thought.
I wonder why you told friends
you were going to give up, give in, give away
your things. Why did you take what you found
in closets and pockets, ask friends what they needed,
even people on the street, if they wanted
this or that knick-knack you held in your arms?

When you got weaker you checked into hospice
for your last days—breathing in the sunlit room,
clutching *a bowl to hold the sun*
to hold us, hold the petals, the pages
of our stories, the poems, the chorus
we have become.

The Dream of Maggie Tulliver

What greater thing is there
for two human souls, than
to feel that they are joined for life—...
—George Eliot

Water everywhere—from the sky, the river, the fields—
I am in a boat, rowing against the current,
looking for Dorlcote Mill, but catching no glimpse
of it, nor the chestnut tree, the house.
Then I see the roof, building half submerged,
trees splaying in the water, debris collecting
around it. All this time, I am hearing my father's voice
urging me to row, telling me I can do anything.
There was my mother's voice, too, telling me to put on
my bonnet, to change my sodden clothes.
This is all so queer because my father is long dead, and
my mother cannot matter in the life I have now,
far from home with my friends Phillip and Stephen, Cousin Lucy.
My little dog, Yap, is in the boat too and Yap
has been no more for so many years. But here he is
brown and white and dripping wet. His odd black ear
flopping to the side, then pricking up at the sound
of my brother Tom's voice, calling from the top of the mill.
Then Tom is in the boat, pulling hard. But we are stuck
in the current. He calls me Magsie, as he used to,
when he was proud of me years past. Now a boat comes by us,
Stephen and Lucy, Phillip—all shouting to warn us of debris,
but Tom says *Too late.* Too late for us. He throws down

the oars and grabs me. Our boat turns over and we sink
in the swirling water, down among willows and reeds, and we
hold each other down and down and down.

There is no air, only water. It is the happiest moment of my life.

Circe

Lucky for me he left when he did.
Lucky his crew was homesick.
I'd forgotten how to live my life:
how to eat and dress and sleep
and what to do when I wake.
We spent most of our time in bed
where he borrowed my immortality
and I became almost human.

Will he say I was a witch
who kept him under a spell?
In fact, I was the enchanted one.
I wove his tunics, washed his back,
cooked banquets every day.
And his crew, I let them become
whatever they wanted to be.
Some were lions or wolves,
these were happy as swine.

Now I'm free to roam the woods,
and, of course, he left the babies.
They'll keep me busy for years
until, according to Hermes, Ulysses'
oldest boy comes back to marry me.
Twenty years means nothing at all.
It will pass like a ship setting sail.
I have no hope for time.
Except this suddenly ticking heart.

Eros/Venus/Psyche

She always spoiled me.
Everyone said so.
They all knew my mother taught me
to play scandalous tricks—
I learned mischief of every kind
at her hands, sitting in her beautiful lap.
But I, too, was beautiful
the most beautiful boy
the gods had ever seen.
They forgave every horrible prank, the chaos
I created with my little bow and arrows.
I shot everyone, even the highest gods,
infected them with earthly lust.
Sometimes I turned them into flames, birds,
serpents, bulls. I served their bestial
desires, ruined their reputations,
caused laughter and shame to rain on them.
Still they forgave me,
had me sit on their knees while
they kissed my soft cheeks,
smoothed my curls and tickled
until I screamed for them to stop.

It was my mother's fault, of course.
She taught me from the minute
I leapt from her womb, to address slights
to her beauty, carry out her intrigues,
commit indecent acts,
these I did these with pleasure

for Venus, my mother, Goddess of Love.
But with this mortal girl, I was different.
For the first time in my immortal life,
Venus told me one thing and I did another.
She said to shoot my arrows into Psyche,
to make her fall in love with a hideous creature—
but as soon as I saw her, the most beautiful
mortal alive, as beautiful as my own mother,

I felt the sting of my own arrow—
I knew I would marry her myself.
And I did, although I never let her know
she had married a god. I loved her only
in darkness, ashamed of my wings,
my smooth skin, my cherub lips.
I wanted stubble, even a beard.
No more of my mother's sweet milk to keep
me an infant. No more downy wings spun
from her hair, no more kisses from her
honeyed mouth. I wanted to grow up,
have my own wife. To be her equal.
I wanted to be a man.

A Fool's Wisdom

No doubt the world is entirely an imaginary world,
but it is only once removed from the true world.
                    —Isaac Bashevis Singer

I dream one thing, but I forget when I wake.
No doubt it is better to be a fool forever
than for one minute to be evil. So says
the rabbi of Frampol, where I lived all my life
until an evil spirit almost made me commit
one bad act. *Gevalt!* How could I do this?

I left Frampol then, to wander the world
of stories. I told people what I learned
in my life of being an idiot. No one called
me dumbbell or ox anymore. I was just Gimpel,
another *schnorrer* who begged from town to town.
I didn't tell I was an orphan, a baker, a husband,
a father to children I had no role in conceiving.

I told them to accept what they are given,
make the best of it. Me, I was given little,
a life of shame and bullying. I took it
as one must. The town gave me a wife who
was a whore and a shrew, but I loved her
with all my heart. Every curse, every slap
she gave me, I cherished her even more
and waited for the next blow to fall.

I warn you, citizens of the great world
outside Frampol—do not give up hope.

I tell you as an old man—do not ever
disbelieve. For, in the next world, soon
to come, no doubt—everything there
will be real. I tell you now there will be
no deceit, no shame. You will be loved
and honored as I, a lummox, a *schlimazel*
from nowhere, will be treated forever
as a person of truth and substance.

Indigestion

I didn't forget smoking is forbidden on Rosh Hashanah.
I forgot I was a Jew.
            —from a Yiddish joke

Because of indigestion I remember
I'm a Jew. I remember also in the taste
of the *tsimmes* I put together every year.
The sweet potatoes, carrots from the garden,
honey from Wilmer's bees, apples from our orchard,
the once-a-year prunes and brisket of beef.

They cook down into memory:
Aunt Sophie opens the tiny oven
of her miniscule kitchen and out
come *tsimmes* and roast chicken,
lukschen kugel, honey cake.
Aunt Goldie steps off the number four bus
pulling chopped liver from her handbag.
From Jersey come Bertha and Emma and Celia
with *taiglach* and *gefilte* fish.
We drive the old green Packard,
with *challahs* and *kichel* from the bakery,
apples from a farm stand in Hackensack.

On Rosh Hashanah I call my children
to wish them happy new year.
"Good *Yom Tov*," I tell them.
They don't even know what I mean.
"What are you doing tonight?" I ask.
One is studying litigation in Los Angeles,

the other dancing salsa in New York.
I ask what they ate for dinner.
Pizza, they say, from separate coasts,
and I wonder: if they aren't eating
gefilte fish, *tsimmes*, chopped liver, *kugel*,
if they don't have indigestion
will they remember
they are Jews?

Pop's Chock'lit Shop

Archie Comics, 1957

They're all here—
        Archie, Reggie, Jughead,
        Betty, Veronica, Moose—
and there's me, Midge,
        almost invisible next to
        my gigantic, dumbbell boyfriend.
I'm Moose's girl,
        and future battered wife, they think.
        But Moose is big and stupid, not mean,
and I won't marry him anyway.
        I keep quiet and blend in,
        but when I get home
I read, I write, I paint, take snapshots
        with my second-hand Brownie
        camera—nothing any of the more
colorful comic book characters would ever
        think of doing. The girls gossip and preen.
        Boys make stupid jokes while Veronica
plans her next outfit/party/racing car/boyfriend.

Betty's lovesick for Archie,
        she's a loud-mouth good-time girl.
        Not bright, but heart in the right place.
Archie and Reggie are lunkhead rivals for Veronica,
        plotting each other's demise. They order
        their shakes and burgers—
Reggie and Moose have black and white
        sodas and Jughead, if you can believe it,

the only one with a functioning brain,
has malted milk and pizza, waffle fries and a burger.
He's secretly thinking of ways he could
make himself famous while still preserving
his goofball image. By the time they're done,
I'm out the door, my coffee-to-go in a brown
paper bag and already writing the next-to-last
chapter of my blockbuster spymaster novel.

The Beautiful Cars

after Robert Frank's photograph
"Public Park, Ann Arbor, MI"

They lounge under the trees—
two-toned Buicks, Pontiacs,
Oldsmobiles, waxed and buffed
and simonized, they are glamorous,
like movie stars waiting for their
close-up, holding still so nothing
will ruin their makeup. The cars
are watchful, smug, on guard
while they pose for the camera.
They are smitten with themselves,
with their chrome and their metallic
paint, their smiling bumpers and
their portholes like perfect smoke
rings running down their fenders.

The cars are vain and lazy. They prefer
to pose where they can be admired.
They dislike heavy feet mashing
their pedals. They shrink from sweaty
hands on their perfect steering wheels.
They are disdainful of the road where
they are expected to perform, to spin
their immaculate white-walled tires
to take greasy oil into their gleaming
engines. They are forced to obey

reductive road signs that trivialize
their every movement, that imply they
are machines that simply stop and go.

The beautiful cars don't like each other.
Some are jealous of the Buick's two-tone
paint job, the Pontiac's deco trim, the sexy
bedroom headlights of Oldsmobiles. They
spew each other with exhaust, drop their
mufflers, hurl curses concerning vulnerable
inner parts, make fun of rising numbers on
odometers, a widening radius of an aging
steering wheel, the sibilant shriek of brakes
that sport last season's shoes. Sometimes
they play tricks—remove gas pedals, lock
doors, siphon gas. The beautiful cars have
no mercy. They love the crazy zig-zag lindy hop
of a blowout, get a rush watching head-on
collisions. They aren't responsible for mishaps.
The beautiful cars are mean and hate their drivers.

History of the Main Complaint

after William Kentridge

1.

In Johannesburg, a man puts a coffee
cup to his ear and sees the world. I sit in
my kitchen in flowered pajamas, sipping
a coffee cup brimming with fear.
Kentridge has drawn the man naked—himself,
an artist—vulnerable, his fear and longing
exposed. He turns on the faucet and water fills
the room, rushes under the door into the street,
where people form lines, something in their eyes
like defiance. They are waiting for something
to happen. In the film, blood runs from the faucet
into the street where police shoot rifles into
the crowd. People are falling. Blood seeps from
their slowly-opening wounds. Blood fills the frame
while a black cat walks through the crowd like time
passing, as though history has already happened.
I sip my coffee waiting for an era to pass, the time
in which I counted, which came back to me
as a gift. Gifts can't be counted on; but once they
are received you think they are yours forever.

2.

A fat man in a business suit is sitting at a desk,
smoking cigars and answering telephones. His suit
is like armor. Nothing from the outside world
can touch him. I wait for my cell phone to bring
me bad news, I am wearing no armor, but cotton
pajamas to cover my heart. As each telephone
rings, the man in the film picks up the receiver.
He blows smoke into each mouthpiece. The cat,
history, sits on the desk of the man in the film
and he strokes it. I am waiting to outlive my own
history, the time I waited to come around again,
the time in which I knew how to matter. Kentridge
draws blue lines through the frame of the film,
connections that bisect the desk, the room,
the building, the street. The lines rise into the sky
where they become constellations resembling
the man who put the cup to his ear. The constellation
dissolves into home; veldt, barn, pond, rock,
utility tower. The man is back where his history started.

3.

The man in the business suit is eating
an enormous meal by himself. The table
in front of him, crowded with roasted
chickens, whole fish, fruit, vegetables,
is set with four glasses of wine. Outside
the building, a line of people shuffle
their feet and groan as their stomachs
rumble. My toast pops out of the toaster
and I scrape some butter over its surface.
The cell phone rings and I answer at once,
an appointment confirmed for later today.
The man in a suit drinks from all four glasses.
He eats the entire chicken, the fish, potatoes.
The line outside grows longer now, with more
rumbling of stomachs and cries for food.
The man in a suit devours some cake
and pie, then pulls a coffee press toward him.
Outside, there are even more people.
The coffee press rings and a handkerchief
in the man's pocket begins to weep. The man
in the suit rises from the table to feed the hungry.
He takes his empty plates to the window,
throws piles of bones down to the crowd.

Washington Heights, 1952

The women are in the kitchen, wearing gingham aprons.

The men are in the dining room, in shirtsleeves. Their ties are loosened and so are their tongues.

Except the old man in the living room.

The women are in the kitchen, seven of them, all sisters. The old man is their father.

The men are in the dining room telling stories the child doesn't want to hear.

The old man is in the living room. He is smoking cigarettes in a long black holder.

And the child?

The women are in the kitchen, washing dishes, telling stories. One is the child's grandmother.

The men are in the dining room, drinking schnapps. Big wet circles form on the backs of their shirts.

The old man is on the green sofa. He wears a navy suit and polka-dot tie. In his pocket are cigarette lighters. One, plain silver, is just for the men. Another, gold with rhinestones, is only for the ladies. His daughters laugh. Ninety-two years old, he still has an eye for the ladies.

The child is in the living room. Her party dress is navy taffeta. Her hair is braided down her back and tied with a ribbon. Over the dress is an apron like her grandmother's, gingham with an embroidered apple for the pocket.

The pillows on the sofa are rose, mustard and blue. The old man motions the child to sit. She has brought him his tea in a glass.

The women in the kitchen are drinking ginger ale now. They laugh about the housekeeper who cleans their father's apartment. "He pinched me," the housekeeper said. "He pinched me you know where!"

In the dining room, some uncles are taking out their handkerchiefs. They mop foreheads and fold up the handkerchiefs. Their gargling voices echo down the hall.

On the living room wall is a painting of a rooster in front of a hen house. Behind the hen house is a hayfield, and then there are woods.

The old man sips his tea from a glass. He sucks it through sugar cubes held in his teeth. He tells the child come closer, pulls her to him on the green couch.

The child watches the rooster in the painting. He crows at daybreak, waking the chickens.

The women are in the kitchen. They don't wonder about the child, who spends weekends there. She plays for hours by herself. None of the women think about the old man. In their sixties now, they don't remember how their father was. They only tell stories about the mother.

The men are in the dining room, lighting up cigars. They tell jokes about "broads" and "tomatoes."

One uncle tells about the second grade in Brooklyn—a teacher so beautiful, she hit him with a ruler and it gave him chills of pleasure.

Another uncle tells about the union and the bosses. One is a *goniff*. Another a *shnorrer*. There are *shvarzes* in the union. You have to watch they don't take the jobs.

In the kitchen, the women are putting on lipstick. They empty the ashtrays and put away dishes.

The men in the dining room put on their jackets. They make knots in their ties, but they don't tie them tight.

The child and the old man are still on the sofa. His hand is creeping under her dress.

"Too tight," he tells her. "Too tight, the underpants. Loosen the elastic, it shouldn't stop the breathing."

She tries to get up, to go back in the kitchen. She liked bringing the tea but doesn't want to stay.

In the painting on the wall it is getting to be daybreak.

The great-grandfather's hand is cold on her belly. His fingers claw at places the child has never touched.

"Don't tell," the old man whispers. "Don't tell we do like this."

What shouldn't she tell? What is it they are doing? Who would she tell anyway, and what words would she use?

The rooster in the painting is crowing too loudly. The sun is screaming, like an alarm. Like the air raid siren in kindergarten when the boys and girls go into the hallway and put coats on their heads to save them from atomic bombs.

The child runs from the living room into the foyer to her coat on the love-seat, small and brown, among the fur coats of the great-aunts, the huge coats of the great-uncles.

The women come into the foyer with shoes on. Their lipstick is freshened. Their faces are powdered. How late it is! Past the child's bedtime. The buses are running but soon they will stop.

The child is asleep on the love-seat, her legs under the coats of the uncles, her arms hugging the coats of the aunts.

They're all laughing now, the men and the women. All in the foyer making plans for next time.

"Friday at my house. I'll give you chopped liver. Next week Gussie's. She can make flanken."

The old man stands in the foyer, in shiny black shoes and his three-piece suit. From under the child the aunts pull his coat. In goes the left arm. Then he changes the cigarette holder from right to left. And puts the right arm into the sleeve.

The child stirs on the love-seat fortress of coats. She imagines the apple on the pocket of her apron is growing in the orchard on the farm in the painting where the rooster is crowing on the living room wall.

The aunts uncover the child in her fortress. "Get up, lazybones. Kiss Papa good-bye."

The great-grandfather takes the cigarette out of his mouth, and drops hot ashes onto her dress. A small hole appears on the taffeta shoulder. The child pulls her breath in. The man's breath is warm. He's bending and putting his mouth near her ear.

"Don't tell," the great-grandfather says. And she doesn't. Until many years later.

Until everyone else in this story is dead.

Until now.

Susan Thomas' first book, *State of Blessed Gluttony* (Red
Hen Press, 2004), was chosen for the Benjamin Saltman Prize
by Phillip Levine and Wanda Coleman. She has also won first
prizes from the *Iowa Poetry Review*, USC (Ann Stanford
Prize), *Spoon River Review*, and *Mississippi Review*. Her
poetry collections, *The Empty Notebook Interrogates Itself*
(2011) and *In the Sadness Museum* (2017) were published
by Fomite Press. She has also published two chapbooks and
a collection of short stories, *Among Angelic Orders* (Fomite
Press, 2014), and is co-translator with Richard Jackson and
Deborah Brown, of *Last Voyage* (Red Hen Press, 2010), a
collection of Giovanni Pascoli's selected poems. Her latest
book is *Take Five* (Finishing Line Press, 2020), a collection of
prose poems with Richard Jackson, Deborah Brown, Barbara
Carlson, and Laura Baird.

Seth Steinzor — *Once Was Lost*
Seth Steinzor — *To Join the Lost*
Susan Thomas — *In the Sadness Museum*
Susan Thomas — *Silent Acts*
Susan Thomas — *The Empty Notebook Interrogates Itself*
Sharon Webster — *Everyone Lives Here*
Tony Whedon — *The Tres Riches Heures*
Tony Whedon — *The Falkland Quartet*
Claire Zoghb — *Dispatches from Everest*

Dual Language
Vito Bonito/Alison Grimaldi Donahue — *Soffiata Via/Blown Away*
Antonello Borra/Blossom Kirschenbaum — *Alfabestiario*
Antonello Borra/Blossom Kirschenbaum — *AlphaBetaBestiaro*
Antonello Borra/Anis Memon — *Fabbrica delle idee/The Factory of Ideas*
Tina Escaja/Mark Eisner — *Caida Libre/Free Fall*
Luigi Fontanella/Giorgio Mobili — *L'Adoescenza e la note/Adolescence and Night*
Aristea Papalexandrou/Philip Ramp —*Μας προσπερνά/It's Overtaking Us*
Katerina Anghelaki-Rooke//Philip Ramp — *Losing Appetite for Existence*
Jeannette Clariond/Lawrence Schimel — *Desert Memory*
Mikis Theodoraksi/Gail Holst-Warhaft — *The House with the Scorpions*
Paolo Valesio/Todd Portnowitz — *La Mezzanotte di Spoleto/Midnight in Spoleto*

Writing a review on social media sites for readers will help the progress of independent publishing. To submit a review, go to the book page on any of the sites and follow the links for reviews. Books from independent presses rely on reader-to-reader communications.

For more information or to order any of our books, visit:
http://www.fomitepress.com/our-books.html

www.ingramcontent.com/pod-product-compliance
Lightning Source LLC
Chambersburg PA
CBHW031445120626
46545CB00006B/2554